Cursive Handwriting Practice Workbook for Teens

Julie Harper

Cursive Handwriting Practice Workbook for Teens by Julie Harper

Children's Books > Education & Reference > Words & Language

Teens > Education & Reference > Language Arts

ISBN 10: 1492230235

EAN 13: 978-1492230236

Table of Contents

Introduction

The goal of this workbook is to inspire teens' interest in learning and practicing cursive handwriting. Teens enjoy reading phrases they can relate to like "talk to you later" and statements like, "Wizard school is so cool." Exercises like these help to make learning fun, whether in the classroom or at home.

This Cursive Handwriting Practice Workbook for Teens focuses on writing phrases and sentences in cursive. Students who need more practice writing individual letters or single words may benefit from using this workbook in combination with a basic cursive writing workbook which focuses on practicing letters and short words.

Three sections of this workbook help students develop their cursive writing skills in three parts:
- ✓ Students practice tracing and copying phrases and sentences in Part 1.
- ✓ Part 2 just involves copying – no tracing.
- ✓ A challenge is presented in Part 3. Here, the sentences are given in print and students must rewrite them in cursive. They can check their answers at the back of the book.

May your students or children improve their handwriting skills and enjoy reading and writing these teen phrases and sentences.

Uppercase Cursive Alphabet

A B C D E F

G H I J K L

M N O P Q R

S T U V W X

Y Z

Lowercase Cursive Alphabet

a   b   c   d   e   f

g   h   i   j   k   l

m   n   o   p   q   r

s   t   u   v   w   x

y   z

Part 1 Trace & Copy

Part 1 Instructions: First trace each word and then copy the words onto the
blank line below.

Teen spirit rules!

Chill out.

Just dance!

Chocoholic here.

Zumba

_____

- - - - - - - - - - - - - - - - - - -

_____

Vogue

_____

- - - - - - - - - - - - - - - - - - -

_____

Interpretive

_____

- - - - - - - - - - - - - - - - - - -

_____

Breakdance

_____

- - - - - - - - - - - - - - - - - - -

_____

Gangnam

_____

- - - - - - - - - - - - - - - - - - -

_____

Best friends forever!

Sleep late on Saturday.

Without a doubt!

A little space, please.

Privacy, for sure!

Skateboarding

Parachuting

Whitewater rafting

Surfing

Bungee jumping

Seriously? That's so eighties.

Don't procrastinate!

You rock! Teen power!

It's a happy day for us!

Don't even think about it.

Hip hop

_____
- - - - - - - - - - - - - - - - -
_____

Pop rock

_____
- - - - - - - - - - - - - - - - -
_____

New wave

_____
- - - - - - - - - - - - - - - - -
_____

Jazz and blues

_____
- - - - - - - - - - - - - - - - -
_____

Rock 'n' roll

_____
- - - - - - - - - - - - - - - - -
_____

Fairy tale romance

No heartaches

Secret crush

You're blushing!

First kiss

Magical

Supernatural

Phenomenal

Druidical

Haunted

Wizard games on Monday

Werewolf race on Tuesday

Vampire tag on Wednesday

Mermaid swim on Thursday

Zombie run on Friday

Carefree times ahead.

Quiet, please.

It's a breeze.

No monkey business!

So far, so good.

Peace and love!

Follow your heart!

Smile brightly.

You make me laugh.

Sunny happy days!

Text me.

Got your number.

What's your e-mail?

Do you Skype?

Cool cell phone case!

Latest and greatest

Fashion police

Glitz and glamour

Trending now

Funky music

Blue-jeans and t-shirt

- - - - - - - - - - - - - - - -

Tuxedo and tie

- - - - - - - - - - - - - - - -

Accessorize

- - - - - - - - - - - - - - - -

Cool sunglasses

- - - - - - - - - - - - - - - -

Summer dress

- - - - - - - - - - - - - - - -

Meet me at the mall.

Hang out with friends.

Tomorrow is movie night.

Come to the pizza parlor.

Hang out at the skate park.

Secret spellbook

Magic potions

Lucky charms

Buried treasure

Hidden chamber

Retweet my message.

_____

- -

_____

Follow my blog.

_____

- -

_____

Like me on Facebook.

_____

- -

_____

Pin me at Pinterest.

_____

- -

_____

Check out my website.

_____

- -

_____

Shooting star

Genie in a bottle

Four-leaf clover

Wishbone

Horseshoe

Didn't mean to do that...

Say it isn't so.

Just be yourself.

Have fun and be silly.

Did I say that?

Tennis anyone?

Love, deuce, ace

Smashing serve!

Lob, volley

Forehand or backhand

Surf the web.

Chat online.

Browse videos at YouTube.

Share photos with friends.

Look it up on Google.

Where's my dream car?

Fuel efficiency is a must.

Reliability and safety, too.

Four-cylinders, six-speed

Maybe a muscle car!

Protect the environment!

Recycle and reuse.

Adopt a pet.

Conserve energy.

Walk, or ride your bike.

No way! Get out of here.

Make a statement.

Give me a break!

Talk to you later.

I'm discombobulated.

Is it Friday yet?

Top of the class!

We're in the party zone!

Seal the deal!

Volunteer. Help someone.

Forever friends

What's your number?

I know this is true love.

Believe in yourself!

Message in a bottle

Wizard school is so cool.

I love learning new spells.

Potions is my hardest class.

We fly brooms in P.E.

Off to become a wizard!

I thought Π was a dessert!

What's trending now?

Failure is not an option!

Who's in charge?

How sweet it is!

Don't feed the zombies.

Don't knock on the coffins.

Quiet during haunting hour.

Stay inside on full moons.

Don't touch the brooms.

It's not worth the trouble.

Is anybody listening?

Why do I even bother?

Come back to earth.

Who's out there? Anyone?

All-star teenager here.

You are looking at a legend.

Work hard. Make history.

You're bursting with talent.

Our future is so bright.

Who needs sleep?

Can you keep a secret?

Why even bother?

What was I thinking?

How did that happen?

Mars needs teenagers.

You're out of this world.

Send me to the moon.

Blast off in ten seconds.

We're headed for the stars.

That sounds so cool.

My fingers are crossed.

Been there, done that.

Pretty please? I promise.

Stick to the facts, please.

So sophisticated!

Bewildered and perplexed!

Electrifying and thrilling!

Cheering and exhilarating!

Rejuvenating!

I'm on cloud nine!

Full of bliss and glee!

So very contented.

I could purr like a kitten!

Such a wonderful life!

Mom loves me the best.

I just want to have fun!

Dad is my ATM machine.

Just follow your heart.

Keep it real.

Part 2 Just Copy

Part 2 Instructions: Copy the phrase or sentence onto the blank line below. In this chapter, there is no tracing.

Snack time: licorice,

malt balls, jelly beans,

ice-cream sandwiches,

pretzels, cookies, and chips.

Fun in the sun!

Flip-flops and tees,

collecting seashells,

boogie boarding, surfing, or

volleyball on the sand.

School dance tonight: Great

music with guest DJ;

plenty of dancing; show

off your new moves; free

punch and snacks, too.

Looking forward to big

events: graduation,

thirteen and sweet sixteen,

semi-formal dance, and

getting my driver's license.

Exciting adventures: Play

paintball with my friends,

go skydiving, try bungee

jumping, go hang-gliding,

or run with the bulls.

If I were a wizard, I would

say, 'Poof!' and my

homework would be done.

I'd have snacks anytime.

I'd win every game.

Weekends are fun!

Saturday morning is for

cereal and cartoons.

Sunday afternoon is for

hanging out with friends.

You're invited to a pizza

party to welcome the

local zombies.

All you can eat pizza

topped with brains.

Has anyone seen my

thinking cap?

I love figuring out puzzles.

How imaginative are you?

I enjoy being creative.

Take me out to the ballgame.

Hot dogs and roasted peanuts.

Base hit, home run, or grand

slam. One, two, three

strikes you're out!

Is a lifeguard on duty?

Let's go deep sea fishing,

whale watching, snorkeling,

scuba diving, ocean

swimming, or boating.

Fun at the amusement

park: loop-the-loop roller

coasters, cotton candy,

water rides, carnival games,

and souvenirs.

Catch me, if you can!

See you at the races.

Don't get lapped.

Professional races are

high-performance.

Gather at a campfire:

Roast marshmallows, tell

ghost stories, watch fireflies,

joke and giggle, look at the

stars, and stay warm.

You're never too old for

old-fashioned games:

spin the bottle, Ouija board,

truth or dare, cards, or even

rock, paper, and scissors.

Snowy days on the

mountain are good for

snowboarding and skiing.

Then meet me at the lodge

for a hot chocolate.

Themed parties are cool:

Hawaiian luau, pizza,

masquerade, pool party,

dance competition, or a

backyard movie.

Supernatural phenomena:

psychic powers, telekinesis,

Bigfoot, ghosts, magic,

unidentified flying objects,

and extrasensory perception.

Run through the

sprinklers on a hot, sunny

afternoon in August.

Go swimming in a

river or pond.

Aaarrrggghhh!

Ahoy, mateys!

Yo ho ho, 'tis a pirate's life.

Jolly Roger, Black Beard,

and Captain Kidd.

Let's spend the day at the

zoo watching the animals:

hippopotamus, cheetah,

lion, zebra, tiger, gorilla,

monkey, alligator, and bear.

Wouldn't it be fun to

spend a full day at the

movies? I could watch

one movie after another!

Don't forget the popcorn.

Saturday is a good day to

hangout at the mall with

my friends. We window-

shop and grab a bite to eat

at the food court.

Walking barefoot through

the grass at the park.

Ready for grilled burgers

and hot dogs with all

the trimmings.

On a hot summer day,

it's fun to play water

balloon volleyball in the

pool. The guys try to empty

the pool doing cannonballs.

We are number one!

Let's go team!

V is for victory!

Teamwork and team spirit

go hand-in-hand!

Inquiring minds want to

know everything!

Curiosity may have killed

the cat, but what fun would

he have had without it?

Do you want to dance?

Ballroom dancing, jazz,

hip-hop, tap, modern,

country and western, folk,

Latin, or punk?

We proved ourselves!

Strong and proud knowing

we could do it!

Go teen girls!

Go teen boys!

Video games at my house

tomorrow: arcade style,

online gaming, three-D,

motion sensor remotes,

aerobic, or team play.

Honk, honk!

Countdown to the day

I get my driver's license!

Beep, beep!

Beep, beep!

Fashion on the runway:

supermodels, lipstick, make-

up, glamour, high heels,

spectacular clothes, poise,

and matching accessories.

Dreams can come true!

Expect more!

Don't worry – be happy.

Work for it.

Think and be positive.

Just between you and me.

I was wondering if

you can keep a secret?

Time will tell!

Yeah! Sure!

Got nothing but love for

you! I will love you

forever and ever!

Love is in the air!

Hugs and kisses.

Spare me the details!

It's not funny!

Are you kidding?

If you know what I mean.

Give me a break!

Grin and bear it!

Chuckle and grin!

For real though!

How cool is that?

Surprise me!

I found a treasure chest.

It was full of chocolate

candy wrapped in gold foil.

The chocolate was yummy,

but the gold was fake!

Help organize a zombie

apocalypse survival guide.

Locate your local shelter.

If a zombie bites, bite back.

Zombie proof your room.

After school, I'm going to

my favorite donut shop.

What should I have: A

bearclaw, glazed, long john,

or jelly-filled?

You are my ray of

sunshine. Walk with

me on this beautiful day!

Happiness is having a

friend like you!

What is your favorite

dessert? Ice-cream cone,

hot fudge sundae, brownies,

strawberry shortcake,

cookies, or cheesecake?

Swinging in a hammock

reading a book by my

favorite author.

Daydreaming!

Turning my phone off!

Fun family days at the

beach. Building the

biggest sandcastle!

Taking walks along the

shore as the sun sets.

Horseback riding is relaxing.

Galloping along,

dreaming of days gone by,

and the way it could

have been!

Dancing in the rain!

Singing my favorite song!

Living for the moment!

Being young and

enjoying life!

Tell me it isn't so!

Courage and strength!

Adventurousness!

Being brave and bold, and

having no regrets.

Country fair days are here.

Deep fried ice-cream,

cotton candy, candy apples,

fun house, prizes, and

the double Ferris wheel.

After school sports:

track and field, hockey,

football, soccer, tennis,

basketball, volleyball, and

swimming. Rah! Rah!

I run with the zombies,

but only when there is

a full moon.

Please, don't wake the

vampires up!

Things to do on a rainy

day: write a poem,

put together a thousand

piece puzzle, solve a cross-

word puzzle, or read a book.

Are you superstitious?

Do you dread Friday the

thirteenth? Knock on wood,

or carry a rabbit's foot

for good luck?

Zombie Movie Guide:

Night of the Living Dead

Dawn of the Dead

The Walking Dead

World War Z

Magical spells, charms,

sorcery, witchcraft,

folklore, incantations,

supernatural powers,

and potions.

Which musical instrument

can you play? The violin,

saxophone, piano, guitar,

organ, clarinet, drums,

harmonica, or trombone?

Seriously, a werewolf ate

my homework!

Have you hugged your

zombie today?

Just don't get bit!

My dog takes me for a

walk every evening.

Sometimes we stop at

the neighborhood dog park.

Woof! Woof!

Part 3 Rewrite Print in Cursive

Part 3 Instructions: Rewrite these phrases or sentences on the blank lines in cursive. Refer to pages 5 and 6 if you need help remembering what the cursive letters look like. Check your answers to Part 3 at the end of the book to make sure you are practicing correctly.

Private: Keep Out!

This means you.

Spooky Halloween fun!

Running with the zombies!

Hungry corpses!

Oh no! What do they eat?

Faster, feet, faster!

Dancing in the rain.

Splishing and splashing!

Slip and slide in the mud.

Thunder and lightning.

Uh oh! No umbrella.

Pirates, parrots, and planks.

Crossbones and skulls.

Peg legs and hooks, too.

Buried treasure!

X marks the spot.

Listening to my playlist!

Turn up the volume!

Singing along

at the top of my lungs!

It's exhilarating!

Inspirational!

_____
- - - - - - - - - - - - -
_____

Be kind and helpful!

_____
- - - - - - - - - - - - -
_____

Don't add to the rumor mill.

_____
- - - - - - - - - - - - -
_____

Follow your heart!

_____
- - - - - - - - - - - - -
_____

Love and serenity.

_____
- - - - - - - - - - - - -
_____

Romantic at heart!

Cherished forever!

Secret love messages!

First impressions!

Respect and admiration!

Start your engines.

Sprint kart, formula,

stock car, monster truck,

off-road, sports car, drag,

and motorcycle racing.

Hit it out of the park!

Throw a curve ball.

Steal a base.

Caught in a pickle.

Call to the bullpen.

Teenager on board.

Mom's taxi service.

Driver's education class.

Four-wheel independence.

Keep it shiny!

The monster ball:

zombie zumba, vampire

tango, werewolf limbo,

ogre breakdancing, and

the witches waltz.

Mr. Disc Jockey, please

play my favorite song.

Will it be rock and roll,

rhythm and blues, pop rock,

jazz, or rap?

Move the ball! Rah!

Offense and defense.

Get a touchdown!

Sack the quarterback.

Block the kicker.

Awesome teenagers!

Every day is a good day!

Hanging with friends.

Giggling and laughing!

Who is your idol?

Best in class!

_____

- - - - - - - - - - - - - - - - - -

_____

Year of the super teen!

_____

- - - - - - - - - - - - - - - - - -

_____

Great accomplishments!

_____

- - - - - - - - - - - - - - - - - -

_____

Victorious.

_____

- - - - - - - - - - - - - - - - - -

_____

Honor roll.

_____

- - - - - - - - - - - - - - - - - -

_____

Hair dye, piercings,

tattoos, make-up,

manicure, pedicure,

braces, contacts,

perfume, and cologne.

Valentine's Day:

one dozen roses,

box of chocolates,

sweet teddy bear,

and secret admirer.

Got my new cell phone!

Includes texting and

internet service.

Built-in camera, too.

What's your number?

I'd rather be reading!

Proud to be a bookworm!

Where's my e-reader?

Any reading is good reading!

Twenty-four hour library.

Waterskiing at the lake.

Swimming at the beach.

Playing frisbee at the park.

Canoeing down the river.

Just enjoying my summer!

Friendship is special.

Always there for each

other; someone to talk

with; got your back;

fun times ahead.

Check out those shoes:

sneakers, cowboy boots,

high heels, sandals,

high-tops, dress shoes,

and flip flops.

Get your yearbook:

classmate photos,

sports, clubs, teachers,

recognition and awards.

How will you sign them?

It's been fun!

Now it's time to go.

Maybe we'll meet again.

Better luck next time.

See you later.

Hooray! I did it!

_____

- -

_____

Congratulations!

_____

- -

_____

Way to go! Awesome job!

_____

- -

_____

Good-bye! See you later!

_____

- -

_____

Sign your name below:

_____

- -

_____

Answers to Part 3

Page 101:
Line 1. Private: Keep out!
Line 2. This means you.
Page 102:
Line 1. Spooky Halloween fun!
Line 2. Running with the zombies!
Line 3. Hungry corpses!
Line 4. Oh no! What do they eat?
Line 5. Faster, feet, faster!
Page 103:
Line 1. Dancing in the rain.
Line 2. Splishing and splashing!
Line 3. Slip and slide in the mud.
Line 4. Thunder and lightning.
Line 5. Uh oh! No umbrella.
Page 104
Line 1. Pirates, parrots, and planks.
Line 2. Crossbones and skulls.
Line 3. Peg legs and hooks, too.
Line 4. Buried treasure!
Line 5. X marks the spot.

Page 105:
Line 1. Listening to my playlist!
Line 2. Turn up the volume!
Line 3. Singing along
Line 4. at the top of my lungs!
Line 5. It's exhilarating!

Page 106:
Line 1. Inspirational!
Line 2. Be kind and helpful!
Line 3. Don't add to the rumor mill.
Line 4. Follow your heart!
Line 5. Love and serenity.

Page 107:
Line 1. Romantic at heart!
Line 2. Cherished forever!
Line 3. Secret love messages!
Line 4. First impressions!
Line 5. Respect and admiration!

Page 108:
Line 1. Start your engines.
Line 2. Sprint kart, formula,
Line 3. stock car, monster truck,
Line 4. off-road, sports car, drag,
Line 5. and motorcycle racing.

Page 109:
Line 1. Hit it out of the park!
Line 2. Throw a curveball.
Line 3. Steal a base.
Line 4. Caught in a pickle.
Line 5. Call to the bullpen.
Page 110:
Line 1. Teenager on board.
Line 2. Mom's taxi service.
Line 3. Driver's education class.
Line 4. Four-wheel independence.
Line 5. Keep it shiny!
Page 111:
Line 1. The monster ball:
Line 2. zombie zumba, vampire
Line 3. tango, werewolf limbo,
Line 4. ogre breakdancing, and
Line 5. the witches waltz.
Page 112:
Line 1. Mr. Disc Jockey, please
Line 2. play my favorite song.
Line 3. Will it be rock and roll,
Line 4. rhythm and blues, pop rock,
Line 5. jazz, or rap?

Page 113:

Line 1. Move the ball! Rah!

Line 2. Offense and defense.

Line 3. Get a touchdown!

Line 4. Sack the quarterback.

Line 5. Block the kicker.

Page 114:

Line 1. Awesome teenagers!

Line 2. Every day is a good day!

Line 3. Hanging with friends.

Line 4. Giggling and laughing!

Line 5. Who is your idol?

Page 115:

Line 1. Best in class!

Line 2. Year of the super teen!

Line 3. Great accomplishments!

Line 4. Victorious.

Line 5. Honor roll.

Page 116:

Line 1. Hair dye, piercings,

Line 2. tattoos, make-up,

Line 3. manicure, pedicure,

Line 4. braces, contacts,

Line 5. perfume, and cologne.

Page 117:

Line 1. Valentine's Day:

Line 2. one dozen roses,

Line 3. box of chocolates,

Line 4. sweet teddy bear,

Line 5. and secret admirer.

Page 118:

Line 1. Got my new cell phone!

Line 2. Includes texting and

Line 3. internet service.

Line 4. Built-in camera, too!

Line 5. What's your number?

Page 119:

Line 1. I'd rather be reading!

Line 2. Proud to be a bookworm!

Line 3. Where's my e-reader?

Line 4. Any reading is good reading!

Line 5. Twenty-four hour library.

Page 120:

Line 1. Waterskiing at the lake.

Line 2. Swimming at the beach.

Line 3. Playing frisbee at the park.

Line 4. Canoeing down the river.

Line 5. Just enjoying my summer!

Page 121:
Line 1. Friendship is special.
Line 2. Always there for each
Line 3. other; someone to talk
Line 4. with; got your back;
Line 5. fun times ahead.
Page 122:
Line 1. Check out those shoes:
Line 2. sneakers, cowboy boots,
Line 3. high heels, sandals,
Line 4. high-tops, dress shoes,
Line 5. and flip flops.
Page 123:
Line 1. Get your yearbook:
Line 2. classmate photos,
Line 3. sports, clubs, teachers,
Line 4. recognition, and awards.
Line 5. How will you sign them?
Page 124:
Line 1. It's been fun!
Line 2. Now it's time to go.
Line 3. Maybe we'll meet again.
Line 4. Better luck next time.
Line 5. See you later.

Page 125:

Line 1. Hooray!   I did it!

Line 2. Congratulations!

Line 3. Way to go!   Awesome job!

Line 4. Good-bye! See you later!

Line 5. Sign your name below:

Other Workbooks by Julie Harper

- Letters, Words, and Silly Phrases Handwriting Workbook (Reproducible): Practice Writing in Cursive (Second and Third Grade).
- Wacky Sentences Handwriting Workbook (Reproducible): Practice Writing in Cursive (Third and Fourth Grade).
- Print Uppercase and Lowercase Letters, Words, and Silly Phrases: Kindergarten and First Grade Writing Practice Workbook (Reproducible).
- Print Wacky Sentences: First and Second Grade Writing Practice Workbook (Reproducible).
- Cursive Handwriting Workbook for Girls.
- Cursive Handwriting Practice Workbook for Teens.
- Spooky Cursive Handwriting Practice Workbook.
- Cursive Handwriting Practice Workbook for Boys.
- Princess Printing Practice Writing Workbook for Girls.
- Sports Printing Practice Writing Workbook for Boys.
- Tongue Twisters Printing Practice Writing Workbook.
- Read Wacky Sentences Basic Reading Comprehension Workbook.
- Wacky Creative Writing Assignments Workbook.